Ruby Tuesday Pear Juice

2 pears, quartered
1 pomegranate
1 apple, quartered

1 Feed the pears through a juicer.

2 Cut the pomegranate in half and scoop out the flesh and seeds. Reserve a few seeds and feed the flesh and remaining seeds through the juicer.

3 Feed the apples through the juicer.

4 Pour into a glass and top with the reserved pomegranate seeds.

Long Ruby Tuesday Juice: Top up the juice with tonic, soda, or sparkling mineral water.

Peach Divine

3 peaches, stoned
1 apple, quartered
1 banana, peeled
½ tsp spirulina, cholorella, or Klamath blue green algae (optional)

1 Place all the ingredients in a blender and blend until smooth.

2 Pour into a glass half-filled with ice.

Peach Divine II: Add 125ml/4floz/½ cup orange juice for a thinner smoothie.

Nectarine Divine: Replace the peaches with nectarines.

Spirulina, cholerella, and Klamath blue green algae, available

from health food shops, contain micronutrients and are sometimes referred to as super foods. They are a perfect addition to morning juices to give a real boost to your body's brain and nervous system.

Super Veg Juice

1 red pepper, seeded and cut into strips
1 yellow pepper, seeded and cut into
strips
Few spinach leaves
2 carrots, trimmed
3 sticks celery
¼ cucumber, peeled

1 Feed the vegetables in the order listed
through a juicer.

2 Pour over ice in a glass.

Super Sweet Veg Juice: Add
1 peeled, cored, and seeded apple
to feed through the juicer.

Carrots are packed with
vitamin A, which will help
your skin stay healthy.

Frozen Berry Smoothie

115g/4oz/1 cup frozen mixed
berries, such as raspberries,
blueberries, and blackberries
225ml/8floz/1 cup milk
4 tbsp whole-milk yogurt
1 tbsp icing (confectioners') sugar

1 Place all the ingredients in a blender and
blend until smooth.

2 If the smoothies are too thick, stir in a
little extra milk.

3 Pour into tall glasses to serve.

Black Forest Berries: Add stoned
cherries to the frozen berry mixture (or
choose a mixture with cherries).

Dairy-Free Berry Smoothie: Replace
the milk with soy milk and yogurt with
50g/2oz/¼ cup silken tofu.

Berries are packed with **antioxidants**. Keep them in the freezer so you can enjoy their benefits any time of the year.

Spice 'n' Tropical

1 wedge pineapple, peeled and cut into chunks
½ small ripe mango, peeled, stoned, and cut into chunks
¼ papaya, peeled, seeded, and cut into chunks
1 small banana, peeled
Juice of ½ lime
Seeds of 3 cardamom pods, lightly crushed
Pinch ground chilli

1 Feed the prepared fruit through a juicer.

2 Stir in the cardamom and chilli, pour into glasses, and serve.

Amazake is made from fermented grains, which convert starches to simpler natural sugars. It can create a sweet creamy texture without added sugar or dairy products.

Amazing Amazake Smoothie

6 to 8 apricots, stoned
125g/4oz/½ cup brown rice amazake
4 tbsp orange juice

1 Place all the ingredients in a blender and blend until smooth.

2 Serve poured over ice.

Amazing Peach Amazake Smoothie: Use 1 ripe peach instead of the apricots.

Amazing Raspberry Amazake Smoothie: Use 50g/2oz/½ cup raspberries in place of the apricots.

Muesli and Apple Smoothie

5 no-soak dried apricots, chopped
5 no-soak dried pitted prunes, chopped
4 tbsp no-added sugar and salt muesli
1 tbsp maple syrup
225ml/8floz/1 cup apple juice

1 Place all the ingredients in a blender.

2 Blend until smooth. Add a little extra apple juice if the smoothie is too thick for your liking.

Warm Muesli and Apple Smoothie: Gently heat the apple juice until just simmering before adding to the blender.

Muesli and Milk Smoothie: Use milk in place of the apple juice.

This smoothie is ideal if you run out of fresh fruit because it uses **nutritious dried fruit.** However, if you do have some fresh berries, add a few to the smoothie to make it even more healthy.

Carrot and Apple Juice

2 large carrots, trimmed
2 apples, cut into wedges

1 Feed the carrots and apples through a juicer.

2 Pour into glasses and serve.

Carrot, Apple, and Celery Juice: Add 2 sticks of celery to the juicer.

night vision booster

Spicy Tomato Juice

8 large ripe tomatoes, quartered

2 carrots, trimmed

4 spring onions (scallions), trimmed

2.5cm/1 inch piece of ginger root, peeled

½ chilli, seeded

1 red pepper, seeded and cut into strips

4 sticks celery

Celery sticks to serve

1 Feed the vegetables in the order listed through a juicer.

2 Pour into glass and serve with celery sticks to stir.

Seedy Tomato Juice: Sprinkle a few mixed seeds such as sesame, pumkin, and sunflower seeds over the drink for extra nutritional benefits.

Easy Tropical

¼ small pineapple, peeled and cut into
   chunks
1 banana, peeled
125ml/4floz/½ cup apple and mango
   juice

1 Reserve a piece of pineapple and a
   slice of banana to decorate if desired.
   Place all the ingredients in a blender and
   blend until smooth.

2 Pour into a glass and decorate with
   the reserved fruit to serve.

Really Tropical: Add ¼ papaya, seeded
and cut into chunks, to
the blender.

Banana and Blueberry Yognog

1 banana, peeled
50g/2oz/½ cup blueberries
225ml/8floz/1 cup natural (plain) yogurt

1 Place all the ingredients in a blender and blend until smooth.

2 Pour into a glass and serve.

Banana and Raspberry Yognog: Use raspberries in place of blueberries.

Oatmeal releases energy slowly. Bananas have simple and complex carbohydrates and give instant energy without the blood sugar crash. This smoothie will keep you going until lunch time.

Banana and Oatmeal Smoothie

1 tbsp fine oatmeal
1 ripe banana
1 tsp clear honey
½ tsp vanilla essence (extract), optional
4 tbsp natural (plain) yogurt

1 Place the oatmeal in a blender and pour in 125ml/4floz/½ cup boiling water. Allow to stand for 10 minutes.

2 Reserve a slice of banana. Place the remainder in the blender with the rest of the ingredients and 125ml/4floz/½ cup cold water. Blend until smooth.

3 Pour into a glass and decorate with the banana slice.

Strawberry and Oatmeal Smoothie: Add 115g/4oz/1 cup strawberries instead of the banana.

Mango Lassi

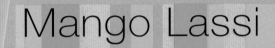

1 ripe mango, peeled, stoned, and cut
   into chunks
350ml/12floz/1½ cups whole-milk
   natural (plain) yogurt
Crushed ice

1 Place the mango and yogurt in a
blender and whiz until smooth.

2 Pour over crushed ice in a glass
to serve.

Banana Lassi: Replace the mango with
1 large, ripe peeled banana.

Spicy Lassi: Add ½ tsp ground
cinnamon and ¼ tsp grated nutmeg
to either the mango or banana lassi.

Banana and Coffee Morning Wake Up

1 ripe banana, peeled
125ml/4floz/½ cup strong hot coffee
125ml/4floz/½ cup hot milk

1 Place the banana in a blender with the coffee and blend until well combined.

2 Carefully add the hot milk and blend briefly to combine.

3 Pour into heat-proof glasses and serve.

Iced Banana and Coffee Wake Up:
Make the coffee and chill well. Proceed as above, adding a handful of ice to the blender with the banana and using chilled milk.

A meal in a glass is an ideal **substitute for breakfast**. The muesli provides quick and slow-release energy, the berries add valuable vitamins, and the yogurt and milk supply calcium.

Breakfast In a Glass

4 tbsp no-added sugar and salt muesli
1 tbsp maple syrup
Few blueberries
Few raspberries
225ml/8oz/1 cup natural (plain) yogurt
125ml/4floz/½ cup skimmed milk

1 Place all the ingredients in a blender and blend until smooth.

2 Pour into a glass and serve.

Pears are great **energizers** because instead of creating a suddern burst of energy, they release energy slowly.

keep on moving

Raspberry, Pear, and Almond Smoothie

2 pears, cut into wedges
1 orange, peeled and segmented
175g/6oz/1½ cups raspberries
4 tbsp ground almonds

1 Feed the pears and orange through a juicer and pour the juice into a blender.

2 Add the raspberries and ground almonds and blend until smooth.

Blackberry, Pear, and Almond Smoothie. Replace the raspberries with blackberries.

Strawberry, Pear, and Almond Smoothie: Replace the raspberries with strawberries.

Pear and Apricot Juice

2 pears, cut into wedges
1 apple, cut into wedges
6 apricots, stoned

1 Feed the fruit through a juicer.

2 Pour into a glass and serve immediately.

Apple and Apricot Juice: Instead of combining pears with an apple, use only apples – you'll need 3 apples.

Spinach and Pepper Punch

150g/5oz/3 cups baby spinach leaves
2 yellow peppers, seeded and cut into
   strips

1 Reserve a couple of strips of pepper.
Feed the spinach and peppers through
a juicer.

2 Pour into glasses and serve with the
reserved sticks of pepper.

Creamy Spinach and Pepper Punch:
Stir the juice into 125ml/4floz/½ cup
natural (plain) yogurt.

This juice is power packed
with vital nutrients, making it a perfect
start to the day.

Strawberry and Vanilla Shake

115g/4oz/1 cup strawberries, washed
   and hulled
225ml/8floz/1 cup milk
4 tbsp vanilla-flavored yogurt
½ tsp vanilla essence (extract)

1 Reserve a strawberry to decorate. Place
all the ingredients in a blender and blend
until smooth. If the smoothie is too thick,
stir in a little extra milk.

2 Pour into a tall glass and decorate with
a strawberry to serve.

Raspberry and Vanilla Shake: Use
raspberries in place of the strawberries.

Blackberry and Vanilla Shake: Use
blackberries in place of the strawberries.

Pineapple and Papaya Power

½ pineapple, peeled and cut into chunks
½ papaya, peeled and cut into chunks
1 apple, quartered

1 Feed the fruit through a juicer.

2 Pour into glasses and serve immediately.

Pineapple Power Smoothie: Blend the pineapple and papaya in a blender with 125ml/4floz/½ cup orange juice.

Nutty Bananas for the Muscles

1 medium banana, peeled
175ml/6floz/¾ cup soy milk
4 tbsp ground almonds
Few ice cubes
Cinnamon stick to serve

1 Place the banana, soy milk, ground almond, and ice cubes in a blender. Blend until smooth.

2 Pour into a glass and add a cinnamon stick to stir.

Bromelain found in pineapple reduces bruising so if you have taken a knock or a fall, try this juice to get you back on your feet.

A perfect drink for before or after **exercise**, wheat germ has the B vitamins, vitamin E, proteins, and minerals. Linseeds have essential fatty acids (good oils), and banana and avocado are good for supplying energy.

Easy Exerciser

2 tbsp wheat germ
1 small banana, peeled
½ avocado, peeled and stoned
125g/4oz/½ cup natural (plain) yogurt
1 tbsp linseeds
2 tbsp lime juice
6 tbsp orange juice

1 Place all the ingredients in a blender and blend until well combined.

2 Pour into a glass and sprinkle with a few more linseeds if desired.

Banana Exerciser: Replace the avocado with ½ of a peeled banana.

Hearty Red Pepper and Sweet Potato

2 red peppers, seeded and cut into strips
1 clove garlic
Few basil leaves
1 medium sweet potato, peeled and cut into chunks
2 carrots

1 Feed the vegetables in the order listed through a juicer.

2 Pour over ice and serve.

Hearty Yellow Pepper and Sweet Potato: Use yellow peppers instead of the red peppers.

Hearty Green Pepper and Sweet Potato: For a slightly sharper juice, use green peppers instead of red peppers.

Sweet potatoes are a rich source of **beta carotene**, which can be converted to vitamin A in the body. They are also packed with vitamin C and potassium. Garlic is good for the **heart**.

Love your Heart

Broccoli has almost as much **calcium** as milk, so this juice is ideal for boosting calcium levels in people on a dairy-free diet. Calcium is an essential aid for women in helping to prevent osteoporosis.

Calcium Booster

175g/6oz/1 cup broccoli florets
2 crisp apples, quartered
1 tbsp lime or lemon juice

1 Feed the broccoli and apples through a juicer and stir in the lime juice.

2 Pour into a glass and serve.

Creamy Calcium Booster: Boost the calcium content further by adding 2 tbsp natural (plain) yogurt.

½ cucumber, peeled
1 avocado, peeled and stoned
Celery stick to stir

1 Feed the cucumber through a juicer.

2 Place the juice and the avocado in a blender and blend until smooth.

3 Pour into a glass, add the celery stick, and serve immediately.

Cucumber can help **lower blood pressure.** As well as being important for cardiovascular health, the avocado may also help to keep you looking good – it is packed with vitamin E, which is good for the skin.

Purple Power

½ small red cabbage, thickly shredded
2 pears, quartered
1 tbsp lemon juice

1 Feed the cabbage and pears through a juicer. Stir in the lemon juice.

2 Pour into glasses and serve.

Fennel Power: Feed ½ a trimmed fennel bulb through the juicer after the pears.

Pears are a great energizer, and they are combined here with red cabbage for a great tasting power juice. Cabbage is loaded with vitamin C, especially red cabbage, and may help prevent colon cancer.

With plenty of the B vitamins, this juice is sure to boost your brain power.

Memory Master

2 fresh dates, stoned and chopped
4 dried apricots, stoned and chopped
2 tbsp seedless raisins
225ml/8floz/1 cup natural (plain) yogurt
1–2 tsp brewer's yeast

1 Place the dates, apricots, and raisins in a blender with 6 tbsp water and purée until smooth.

2 Add the yogurt and brewer's yeast and blend again.

3 Pour into a glass and serve.

Wheat Master: Replace the brewer's yeast with wheat germ.

Pineapple is a good source of thiamine, riboflavin, and manganese, and these are all important for **energy** production.

On the Go

½ pineapple, peeled and cut into chunks
1 large banana, peeled
115g/4oz/1 cup strawberries, washed
  and hulled

1 Place all the ingredients in a blender and blend until smooth.

2 Pour into glasses and serve.

Stay On the Go: Add to the blender a little cooked brown rice for slow-released energy. Thin with a little water or apple juice if desired.

Sunny Tofu Smoothie

225g/8oz/1 cup soft tofu
225g/8oz/2 cups mixed berries such as
  blackberries, raspberries, strawberries,
  and red or blackcurrants
1 tbsp lime juice
Pineapple juice
1 tbsp sunflower seeds

1 Place the tofu, berries, lime juice, and a splash of pineapple juice in a blender and blend until smooth.

2 Add extra pineapple juice until you have a smoothie of your preferred thickness.

3 Pour into glasses and sprinkle with sunflower seeds to serve.

Orange Tofu Smoothie: Use orange juice in place of the pineapple juice.

Tofu, made from soy beans, is a great vegetarian source of protein and iron, and it has the B vitamins, calcium, potassium, and other minerals, making it an energizing drink.

Try this smoothie for a stress-free start to the day. Avocado contains oleic acid, which is good for the heart. Bananas, which are a rich source of potassium, are good for lowering blood pressure.

Heart Pacer

1 small banana, peeled
1 small avocado, peeled and stoned
1 tbsp clear honey
225ml/8floz/1 cup soy milk
Few raspberries

1 Place the banana and avocado in a blender and blend until smooth.

2 Add the honey and milk; blend again.

3 Pour into glasses and top with a few fresh raspberries.

Heart Pacer with Dates: For an even greater dose of potassium, add a few chopped dates to the blender in step 1.

Blueberry Heart Pacer: Top with a handful of blueberries in place of the raspberries.

Green Surprise

115g/4oz/½ cup broccoli florets
Small handful watercress
Small handful parsley
½ pineapple, peeled and cut into chunks
½–1 tsp spirulina, chlorella, or Klamath blue green algae (optional)

1 Feed the broccoli, watercress, and parsley through a juicer. Follow with the pineapple.

2 Stir in the spirulina, chlorella, or Klamath blue green algae if using.

3 Pour into glasses and serve.

Popeye Surprise: Use spinach instead of the watercress.

This vitality juice will give you strength and energy you never knew you had. Watercress, as well as being good for the hair and nails, has a good supply of iron, magnesium, and calcium. Spirulina, chlorella, and Klamath contain minerals that are often missing from our daily diet.

Sweet Potato and Cabbage Energizer

2 carrots, trimmed
1 small sweet potato, peeled and cut
  into chunks
½ small savoy cabbage, shredded
Handful of seaweed
2 tsp sesame seeds

1 Place the carrots, sweet potato, cabbage, and seaweed in a blender and blend until smooth.

2 Pour into glasses, sprinkle the sesame seeds on top, and serve.

Oriental Energizer: Replace the cabbage with ½ medium head of Chinese cabbage and add a handful of pak choy.

Seaweed is a rich source of minerals and the sesame seeds are an excellent source of energy, making this combination a good drink for anyone who is experiencing stress and fatigue.

This energizing drink is the perfect boost when coping with a work overload. It's packed with vitamins A, C, and E and potassium and will help you to improve your mental capacity to concentrate.

Rocket Booster

2 carrots, trimmed
1 kiwi fruit
1 large tomato
Handful of rocket (arugula)
Handful of watercress
2 apples, quartered

1 Cut two slices from a tomato and reserve. Feed the remaining ingredients through a juicer.

2 Pour into glasses, decorate with the tomato slices, and serve.

Spinach Booster: Replace the rocket (arugula) with a handful of spinach.

Making Simple Juices

Some recipes for smoothies require the addition of fruit juices. You can use shop-bought juices, but if you have a juicer, you may want to make your own fresh juice for your smoothies, or you may simply want to make single fruit juices to drink. Here is a guide to how much juice you will get from the most popular fruit and vegetables.

To make 225ml/8floz/1 cup you will need:

Apple Juice: 4–5 apples
Orange Juice: 3–4 oranges
Pineapple Juice: ½ medium --pineapple
Tomato Juice: 4–6 medium tomatoes
Carrot Juice: 5–6 large carrots
Grapefruit Juice: 2 grapefruit
Grape Juice: 225–300g/8–10oz/
    2–2½ cups grapes
Mango Juice: 1½–2 mangoes
Pear Juice: 4–5 pears
Cherry Juice: 450–500g/1lb–1lb2oz/
    2–2½ cups cherries
Pomegranate Juice: 4–5 pomegranates

Use these quantities only as a guide. These juices were made using a centrifugal juicer (see pages 16–17). If you use a masticating juicer, you will get a larger quantity of juice because these machines are more efficient. Also remember that the amount of juice will vary between the different varieties of the same fruit and even from season to season. Ripe local fruits in season are usually juicier than fruits that have been picked unripe and flown across the world.

Juices Hints and Tips

Recipes make one to two glasses, depending on the size of your glass and the amount you want to drink. In general, vegetable juices are drunk in smaller quantities than fruit juices.

Stick to one type of measuring system. Never switch between them. Cup measurements are for standard American cups.

Always use fruit and vegetables that are in peak condition.

Wash fruit and vegetables well before use.

Prepare fruit and vegetables just before you need them. Some vitamins will start to be destroyed when you cut into the produce, and some fruit and vegetables discolor quickly.

Use organic ingredients if you want to avoid pesticide residues.

Cut vegetables into pieces that can be fed through the juicer's feeding tube easily. This will vary from machine to machine. Some machines will take whole apples, others will need the fruit or vegetables to be cut up in small pieces.

Insert soft fruit such as strawberries and blueberries slowly to extract the most juice. Follow soft fruit and leaves with a harder fruit such as an apple or a vegetable.

If you do need to store the juice, keep it in the refrigerator and add a few drops of lemon juice. (This will keep it from discoloring.)

Serve well chilled – use chilled vegetables and fruit or serve over ice.

Dilute juices for children with an equal quantity of water. You can use sparkling mineral water to create a fizzy fruit drink.

Fruit is high in fructose, a natural sugar, so people with diabetes should not drink too much. Dilute with water if necessary.

Do not drink more than 3 glasses of juice a day unless you are used to it – too much juice can cause an upset stomach.

Very dark vegetables such as beetroot (beet) and broccoli can have strong flavors. Dilute with water or with a milder flavored juice such as apple or celery if you want.

Smoothie Bases

Many smoothies are 100 percent fruit, but to blend efficiently a liquid is often added.

Fruit juice:
In 100 percent fruit smoothies, fruit juice is added if necessary. If you have a juicer, juice your own fruit to maximize the vitamin content (see pages 12–13). For speed or convenience, you can use shop-brought juices. Chilled juices not made from concentrate have the best flavor.

Yogurt:
When yogurt is added as a base it adds valuable calcium to the smoothie. Using a yogurt with live bacteria is good for the digestion, providing healthy bacteria. Greek-style yogurt will give the creamiest results but has the highest calorie content. Whole-milk yogurt can be used as a substitute for Greek-style yogurt. It adds more creaminess to the drink than a low-fat yogurt, with a calorie content that is higher than low-fat yogurt but not as high as Greek-style yogurt. Fruit-flavored yogurt may have a lot of added sugar.

Milk:
Like yogurt, milk added to smoothies provides a good source of calcium. Calcium is important for growing children, and smoothies are a good way of including milk in a fussy child's diet. Whole-fat milk has the most flavor, but for those wishing to reduce fat content, skimmed or semi-skimmed milk is better.

Cream:
For special occasions, adding single (light) or double (heavy) cream to a smoothie will give it a richer flavor.

Crème fraîche, fromage frais, quark, cottage cheese, mascarpone:
These dairy products can be added to smoothies to provide calcium and as thickeners. The fat content varies and those with a high-fat content such as full-fat crème fraîche and mascarpone should be used in moderation. Low-fat crème fraîche, cottage cheese, and fromage frais can be used more frequently. Cottage cheese and other low-fat cheeses also add protein and make a smoothie more filling. They are good additions when a smoothie is being served in place of a full meal.

Ice Cream and sorbet:
These can be added to smoothies for extra creaminess or flavor, as well as to to cool the drink. They can be blended with the fruit or added by the scoop in place of ice.

Dairy substitutes:
Tofu is high in protein and low in fat. It is a good source of calcium and contains vitamin E. It has little flavor but will give your drink a more satisfying thickness and creamy texture.

Soy milk and soy yogurt can also be used as an alternative to dairy products, as can rice milk and oat milk. You can also use coconut milk, banana, and avocado to give smoothies a creamy texture and good flavor.

Smoothie Hints and Tips

Recipes make one to two glasses, depending on the size of your glass and the amount you want to drink.

Stick to one type of measuring system. Never switch between them. Cup measurements are for standard American cups.

Wash fruit and vegetables well. Peel if required and cut into chunks.

Use fruit and vegetables in peak condition.

Prepare fruit and vegetables just before you need them. Some vitamins start to be destroyed as you cut into the produce, and some produce discolors quickly.

Add liquids such as fruit juice, milk, or yogurt to the blender first.

For maximum nutritional benefit, serve the drinks immediately after preparing them.

Smoothies may separate on standing. This does not affect the flavor. Serve with a straw twizzler or spoon to stir before drinking.

Fresh ripe fruit should provide enough natural sweetness, but you can add a little extra sugar or honey to sweeten if required.

Keep berries and chopped up soft fruit such as apricots, peaches, and bananas in the freezer to make instant iced smoothies. They can go into the blender when frozen.

Smoothies are best served cold. Chill the ingredients before use and serve with plenty of ice. Crushed ice will cool a drink quickly. You can also use ice cream or sorbet.

Smoothies tend to be thick, but you can alter the thickness of the drink to your taste. Simply add extra milk, water, or fruit juice to achieve your preferred thickness.

If the smoothie is too thin, add a banana, which is a great thickener, or some frozen ingredients such as frozen fruit or ice cream. Or use cooked rice to thicken the smoothie.

You can remove seeds, pips, or fibrous material from the smoothie by straining through a nylon sieve. This will remove the fibre content, thus affecting the nutritional value of the drink, but it is useful if you find them unpleasant or you have fussy children.

Some liquids increase in volume and froth on blending so never overfill the blender.

Make sure the lid is firmly on your blender before processing.

Wash the blender as soon as possible after use. If fruit becomes dried on, soak in warm soapy water for a few minutes to soften the fruit.

Equipment

Whether you want to make juices, smoothies, or both, there is certain equipment that will be essential to have in your kitchen.

Juices

If you want to make juice from hard fruit and vegetables such as carrots, apples, and pears, you will need to invest in a juicer. There are two main types of juicers available.

Centrifugal juicer: This is the least expensive type and it works by finely grating the fruit or vegetables and then spinning them at high speed to separate the juice from the pulp, which is then discarded.

Masticating juicer: This machine is more efficient, but it comes with a higher price tag. It finely chops the fruit, then forces the juice out through a fine mesh.

Food processor: Some types have a centrifugal juicer attachment. It will not be as efficient as a dedicated machine; however, it will be more than adequate for occasional juicing.

Citrus juicer: Citrus juicer attachments are available for some juicers and food processors. These are specifically designed to squeeze juice from citrus fruit and are the most efficient equipment for juicing this kind of fruit. However, you can squeeze citrus fruit by simply peeling and feeding the segments through the juicers. Alternatively, you may prefer to use a simple hand lemon squeezer or reamer.